I have seen
POMPEII

Mural fresco in the House of the Dioscuri

d'ORIANO editore

INDEX

Historical Notes

The volcanic eruption of 79 AD interrupted dramatically any form of life in Pompeii. In few hours the city was completely buried by several layers of lapilli, volcanic sand and even a layer of pisolite ashes up to an height of about six meters. Many inhabitants were crushed by the roofs which collapsed under the weight of the lapilli, others, instead, died for the gas exhalations given off by Vesuvius. The description of those events in the two letters which Pliny the Younger wrote to Tacitus, a Roman historian, about his uncle Pliny the Elder's heroic death is emotional. At that time he was in command of the fleet which was stationed in Misenum; so when he saw the eruptive phenomenon in the distance he moved towards the Vesuvian area with his ships, both for scientific

Image of the Vesuvio during an eruption.

View of the Roman Forum.

curiosity, and for helping those who were overcome by that tragic event; but in his generous surge he fell victim to gaseous emissions. Pliny's words are corroborated by the casts which they obtained from the victims appearing in the most agonizing attitudes, died at the moment of trying a final flight, protecting themselves from the injurious exhalations with their cloth hem or carrying a precious object or some coins during their flight. The area remained deserted, hiding the effects of the disas-

ter, for about seventeen centuries. Perhaps the place, as long ago as the Middle Ages, began to be called Civita, a characteristic name given, in Southern Italy, to settled areas then abandoned, but nobody

The casts obtained by filling the empties produced by the organic decomposition of the bodies.

View of the Triangular Forum with the monumental stair in the centre linking up the Theatres and the Four side porch from the arcade of the Forum.

thought to identify it with the ancient Pompeii. The city stood on a hill top of volcanic

Panthea hand with representation of various divinity, attributed to the house of Sestilius Pyrricus.

scoriae from which it dominated and defended its river and sea port and also controlled a very important road junction which opened, with its branch lines, inside, towards Campania Felix, and outside, towards the sea. Actually, it seems that right the road axis fostered its growth and development and was the cause of the first nucleus of the future city which was born and expanded as agricultural-trading center before establishing itself industrially with its collateral manifacturings. Its wide, very fertile hinterland sent the agricultural products towards the coast by that vital sap which was the Sarno River, at that time surely navigable, and received and sorted out the luxury, exotic products coming from abroad. The most direct

Via dell'Abbondanza. Below on the left, Porta Nola.

proofs that the heart of that city pulsated frenetically are the furrows left by the cart wheels into the basalt, and today following them it is still possible to reconstruct the city movement of those goods, both at their arrival and their departure, and therefore the organization of the inner life

with more or less residential quarters, pedestrian precincts such as the Civil Forum and more crowded arteries such as Via dell'Abbondanza and Via Stabia, where many shops overlooked like in our modern main streets. In front of those shops, several holes, which pierced the pavement toothing for tethering pack animals, are other proofs of that intensive movement and swarming of life. Few things of the Oscan Pompeii, dating back at least to the 8th century BC, remain: only a pre-Samnite wall

Ruins of the Arcade of Samnite age that encircled the southern side of the Forum.

of the 6th century. As regards the next dominations, that is, the Greek one in the 6th century and from 474 to 425; the Etruscan one from 525 to 474 and the Samnite one, belonged to a remote, little known history. Its entrance in the Roman history was represented by the Samnite wars (310 BC), as ally of Rome, to which it will be faithful until the Punic wars. But, at the outbreak of the social war, (89 BC) Pompeii, which allied itself with the other cities of Campania, was besieged and conquered by Silla. In 80 BC Pompeii became a Roman colony and was called *Cornelia Veneria Pompeiorum Colony*, whose name alluded openly to the dictator who had conquered it and the divinity which was particularly dear to him. It began a period of progressive integration with the Roman regulations and the new Roman families who came to live there. The process of integration between new and old inhabitants was quick and pacific. The city planning development was considerable for the demand of new areas to devote

The Weavers, "fullonica" scene, with mural paintings outside the shop of Verecundus in via dell'Abbondanza.

Detail of the excavation of the House of the Working Painters.

to the growing businesses and handicrafts. The restoration works of the Forum, the Temple of Jove, the theatres and the construction of new public monuments started. A temple in honour of Augustus, another one in honour of Vespasian, the imposing building of Eumachia, the Large Palestra, the Amphitheatre sprang up. In 62 AD Pompeii, together with other cities of Campania, was devasted by a violent earthquake suffering extensive damages. The reconstruction and restoration works appeared expensive and very long to carry out. Plain houses, shops, environments and installations used for job were rebuilt quickly, instead, the reconstruction works of huge, elegant houses, public buildings such as the Forum, the temples and the theatres, went ahead very slowly. Even if Pompei revived more beautiful, i was still a work site when the eruption occured. The discovery of Pompeii was due to the digging of a tunnel beneath the hill of "Civita", arranged by the architect Domenico Fontana between 1600 and 1954, for conveying the waters of the Sarno River. During the dig-

Relieved plate that decorated the "larario" of the house of Lucius Caecilius Iucundus, where is portrayed the collapse during the earthquake of the 62 A.D. Now preserved in the Archaeological Superintendence of Pompei.

Civil Forum, the Arcade.

ging, despite the discovery of inscriptions and buildings with frescoed walls, they did not think right to extend the exploration. Only in 1748, 10 years later the start of the excavations in Herculaneum, under the reign of Charles of Bourbon, the first real exploration began; in 1763, outside Porta Herculaneum, the find of a cippus with the engraving of a decree of Vespasian removed any doubt about the identity of Pompeii. The excavations had a substancial boost in the first half of the 19th century, because, between 1806 and 1832, most public buildings and some great private buildings were brought to light. In 1860 under the supervision of Giuseppe Fiorelli, a phase of methodical, rational excavations began. Among other things, he pioneered the prac-

tice of taking impressions and casts from the victims of the eruption, pouring liquid plaster into the cavity produced in the ash bank by the organic

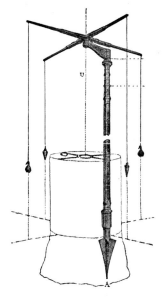

The "groma", that is the square land-surveyor of the geometer Verus.

"Thermopolium". In the panel the ruins of a masonry desk with the "dolia"(jars) already used for the preservation of foods and drinks.

decomposition of the bodies. The division of the urban area in REGIONES (quarters) and INSU-LAE (blocks) was made by Fiorelli following a criterion which was inspired by Ippodamo from Milito, an architect lived in the 5th century BC. The excavatores gave the name to the houses they discovered according to particular criteria: for example, giving them the name of the last dweller after the find of a bronze seal in one of the rooms; the name of some visitor during the excavations; the name of an important artefact, painting or other discoveries in the same houses when there were not information about their dwellers. The streets, paved with basalt around 150 BC and often crossed by big stones for an easier crossing of pedestrians from one side to the other, are all almost rectilinear, with the "DECUMANI" - east-west - and the "CARDINES"-north-south - (the main streets) which crossed at right angle forming an orthogonal mesh. With the growth of the city other two support streets, Via dell'Abbondanza, which represented the new, great, city "decumanus", and via del Foro, which was parallel to Via Stabiana forming another "cardo", were added to the greater "decumanus" formed by Via Nola and the main "cardo" of Via Stabiana. Around those axes a close network streets which had the function of marking the insulae sprang up.

Hydria

Pitcher

Glass

Mortar

View of the Suburban Thermae built in more levels in the sloping area among the walls of the town and the road leading to Porta Marina. Aside, fresco of a maenad. Below, the interior of the Suburban Thermae.

① Suburban Baths

Realized at more levels in an irregular area which extended between the city walls and the road descending from Porta Marina. In this last one the front entrance, composed by a vestibule which leaded to a porticoed triangular area, was sited. On the ground floor there were the thermal rooms; the *apodyterium*

with walls frescoed with numbered erotic paintings, the *frigydarium* and the *natatio* with seascapes and Nilotic scenes painted on the walls. At the corner of the bath there was a nymphaeum with a fountain where the water flowed out from an artificial grotto decorated with a mosaic representing Mars and some amorini. Finally, there were the *tepydarium*, the circular-shaped *laconicum* and the great *calydarium*.

View of Porta Marina. Below, an hypothesis of reconstruction of Porta Marina as it was.

2 Porta Marina
and city walls

A wide, barrel-vaulted arcade crossed by a steep "basolato" street, which came out from the city and leaded to the sea. Constructed in *opus incertum* had two arches; on the left the smallest one for the pedestrian crossing and one for the pedestrian crossing and on the right the biggest one for the passage of carts and pack animals. Laterally to the gate there are ruins of the Samnite ramparts and walls, dating back to the 6th century BC. In the north of the street there are remains of a wide porticoed paviment with square pillars where some shops and the acces to the Suburban Baths opened.

Ruins of the temple of Venus destroyed by the earthquake of 62 A.D.

3 Temple of Venus

Little has been found in this temple, not only because it was still being reconstructed at the time the explosion buried it, but also because it lies within an area where the pillage of the ancient building materials (especially marble) immediately following the eruption was more intense. The temple cell could be seen from the Sarno river and from the sea, so that during the night this sacred spot was also a sort of light-house for boats (probably fires were always kept burning). On the eastern and western sides the cell was surrounded by double colonnades, with a single row of columns on the northern side. The temple was founded during the period of wars around the year 80 B.C. when the dictator Lucius Cornelius Silla subdued Pompeii, making it a roman colony and dedicating it to his patron divinity, Cornelia Veneria Pompeiorum Colony.

Venus on a chariot drawn by elephants; a wall fresco on the external facade of Verecundus's workshop in Via dell'Abbondanza

Crossroads of Via Stabia with Via del Vesuvio in an arc structure.

The Streets

Perhaps it may be hard to imagine that the streets of Pompeii were once thronged with men and women, rather like our own towns. And yet, Pompeii was a throbbing town and, despite the earthquake of 62 B.C., was a crowded commercial centre, where goods and people arrived from the villages and towns nearby. Naturally, the streets made up the scenery for most of this activity. Many inns and shops, somewhat like

Via dell'Abbondanza, sculpture of a penis used to point out the house of Brothel.

Crossway with a public fountain with a square and a sprout decorated in relief.

modern cafes, lined the streets, especially at the major crossroads and in the places where the most people gathered. They met the demand of tradesmen, workers, idlers, or the theatre and amphitheatre crowds, for food and beverages.

Most of the streets of Pompeii were paved with broad stones, irregularly shaped, and were flanked on both sides by high sidewalks. Quite often, between one sidewalk and the other, we find big blocks of stone rising above the street level so that people could get across, especially when the streets were wet and muddy. The streets running north-south are called "cardini" while the "decumani" run eastwest. The main street, or cardo maximus, is Via di

Via Stabia.

Stabia, which links Porta Mercurio with Porta di Stabia. There two decumani. The upper one is made up of Via delle Terme, Via della Fortuna, and Via di Nola; the lower one starts from Porta Marina and crosses over to Porta di Sarno along Via Marina and Via dell' Abbondanza.

Via Mercurio.

Temple of Apollo with the copy of the shooting Apollo. Aside, an hypothesis of reconstruction.

4 Temple of Apollo

We know for certain that this temple was consecrated to Apollo thanks to the dedication in Oscan by quaestor Oppius Campanus that was found in the cell. One enters the scared area form Via Marina through a tuff portal from the Samnite period. Interestingly, the view of this sacred building is blocked by the central column of the portico's short side, which suggests that the main entrance was once directly from the Forum. This hypothesis is confirmed by the fact the main facade of the altar at the bottom of the temple steps faces the Forum. The sacred area is surrounded by a portico with 48 Doric columns in the centre of which, on a podium in the Italic style, is the actual temple. The cell originally contained a statue of a divinity (not found) and a rock of carved tuff representing the *world's navel*, modelled on the one located in the famous sanctuary of Apollo in Delphi. At the bottom of the temple is an altar in Greek Marble dedicated shortly after 80 A.C. by Marcus Portius, Lucius Sestilius, Cneus Cornelius and Aulus Cornelius, quattuorviri of Pompeii. At the top of the Ionic column to the left of the stairway there once was a meridian (sun dial), which the duumviri Lucius Sepunius Sandilianus and Marcus Erennius Epidianus commissioned. The two bronze statues inside the sacred

Fresco of the Vetti's house.

precincts (*Apollo with Bow* to the right and Diana to the left) are copies of the originals (now in the National Museum of Naples) and datable to the late Hellenistic period. The temple of Apollo was also being restored at the time of the eruption. It is one of the oldest temples in the city, Apollo being the main divinity in early Pompeii.

5 Basilica

This is the oldest existing Basilica, dating back to the 2nd century B.C. The seat of the law courts was here and commercial and financial transactions also took place. After a portico comes the main entrance, which opened on the forum and, differently from the majority of basilicas, is located on one of the building's short sides.

The tribunal, part of the Basilica where the law-courts were, was on the short side, opposite the entrance, and consisted in a two meter high podium on top of which were six Corinthian columns. There are no stairs to the podium, this suggests that it could only be reached through wooden stairs, which could be removed in order to separate the judges from the rest of the people. Another hypothesis is that the podium was simply a sacellum for religious statues.

The 28 columns of the portico are made of cut tiles. Judging

Hypothesis of reconstruction of Basilica.

from their diameter they must have been at least eleven meters tall. They probably supported the big beams of the roof, although some believe the central nave of the building was open to the sky. The walls are decorated with panels of painted stucco. The Basilica had two other entrances on the long sides, one looking south and one north on Via Marina.

The sorceress and the wayfarer, Pompeian fresco. Naples, National Archaeological Museum.

In spite of the rigor of the Roman laws, that thought their exercise a punishable criminal action with the exile and even with the death, magic practices flourished.

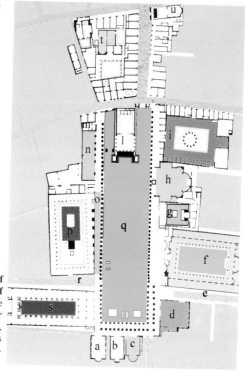

Plant of the Forum and of the public buildings and of cult places, located to the sides of the rectangular area. Below of the right, detail of the Doric columns of the Arcade that surrounded the area of the Forum.

6 Civil Forum

The Forum is a great rectangular square (38 metres of width and 142 metres of length) originally paved with tufa; after the earthquake of 62 BC the paving was remade of travertine. A portico in double order, the lower one Doric and the upper one Ionic, surrounded the Forum on three sides, except the northern side. The square was a pedestrian precinct with the service streets blocked through special rocks. The Forum was the political, economic, commercial, religious center of the city. On the southern side of the portico some monumental bases of imperial hon-

orary statues are visible, while along the porticoes there are some statues of noble citizens. Public, religious, economic

View of the town buildings from the southern side of the civil Forum.

buildings was sited around the Forum, almost hidden by the portico, while the only completely visible building was the Temple of Jove. In the north the Forum is closed by two triumphal brick arches, which at one time were faced with marble.

7 Municipal Buildings

On the southern side of the Forum are three buildings that were the seat of the city administration. The one closest to the Basilica, with a marble pavement and six niches for honorary statues, is where scholars think the Curia was located, a place where a sort of city council gathered. In the central building were the archives where documents relating to the city administration were kept. The third building, which was probably panelled in marble, was occupied by the offices of the duumviri, the highest authority in Pompeii.

8 Comitium

On the south-eastern corner of the Forum is a large building called the Comitium, where elections took place.

It had entrances from Via dell'Abbondanza and the Forum so that the people who had to vote could go in and out of the building in an orderly fashion. A podium on the southern side was presumably used by magistrates whose function was to oversee the elections. This building, too, was lavishly adorned with marble slabs, although at the time of the eruption it was probably still being renovated.

The interior of the Room of the Aediles.

Bronze Oil lamp

Market scene

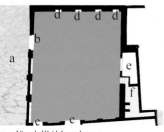

a - *Via dell'Abbondanza*
b - *Entrance in the Comitium from Via dell'Abbondanza* **c** - *Entrances in the Comitium from the civil Forum*
d - *Niches* **e** - *Tribune* **f** - *Services*

EVMACHIAE·L·F
SACERD·PVBL
FVLLONES

⑨ Building of Eumachia

Scholars have identified this building built by Eumachia, priestess of Venus, as the seat of wool market and the dyers' corporation thanks to a statue of Eumachia (now at the National Museum of Naples) dedicated by these artisans. The building, however, probably had other more important public functions as well, given its lavishness and the presence of references to the *Gens Julia*. The four big niches on the façade were probably occupied by the four statues of the ancestors of the imperial family, i.e. Aeneas, Romulus, Julius Caesar, and Augustus, as in the Forum of Augustus in Rome. The building of Eumachia belongs to the Tiberian period (14-37 A.D.). It has an ample central courtyard surrounded by a portico with a double row of columns; in this apse at the back was probably a statue of the Concordia Augusta. The courtyard is surrounded on

Marble door placed in the entrance of the building of Eumachia.

three sides by a corridor with windows and two doors to the left and right of the main entrance. On the short side of this corridor is the spot where Eumachia's statue was found. Finally, one should note the magnificent marble portal decorated with acanthus leaves and little birds.

10 Temple of Vespasian

This temple was certainly built after earthquake of 62 A.D. The entrance is marked by a door after which come four columns. The door leads to a courtyard at the back of which, on top of a podium, is found a cell with the pedestal of a cult statue. In the centre of the sacred area is an altar decorated with marble. On the facade facing the Forum a sacrificial scene is depicted: a priest with his head covered is placing offerings in a tripod while a bull is being brought for the sacrifice.

The temple of Vespasian placed in the centre of the open area. A scene of sacrifice decorated the side of the altar turn toward the Forum.

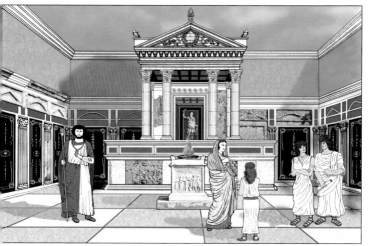

Temple of Vespasian, an hypothesis of reconstruction.

11 Sanctuary of the Public Lares

This building also dates back to the last decades of Pompeii. Here, the official ceremonies in honour of the public Lares, the patron divinities of the city, were held. The statues were presumably located in the various niches found on the side walls and in the great central apse. The building, of which the pavement and walls are lavishly adorned with marble, had a sacrificial altar in the centre of the sacred area that was open to the sky.

12 Macellum

This was the great food market of Pompeii where meat, fish, fruit, vegetables and cereals were sold in shops and stalls. Remains of cereals and fish-bones have been found in the building and in the sewers. The building has three entrances: the main one is from the Forum and leads to a large courtyard with portico. A series of shops are at the back. Those on the opposite side open directly on Via degli Augustali. At the back there is a small sacellum dedicated to the imperial family. In the niches to the right are the moulds of a male and female statue (now in Naples) of members of the imperial family, which have yet to be identified. In the centre is a low

The external of the Macellum seen from the Forum.

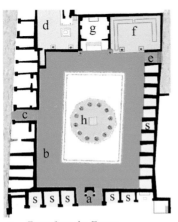

platform with twelve bases on which were placed twelve poles, which in turn supported a wooden roof. In the centre was a fountain used to clean the fish to be sold.

Aside, the ruins of the Tholos for the sale of the fish and the hypothesis of reconstruction.

a - *Entry from the Forum*
b - *Colonnade porticoes*
c - *Entry from Via Agustali*
d - *Meeting area*
e - *Entry from Via del Balcone Pensile*
f - *Local sale of meat and fish*
g - *Sacellum for the imperial cult*
h - *Tholos for the sale of the fish*
s - *Tabernae*

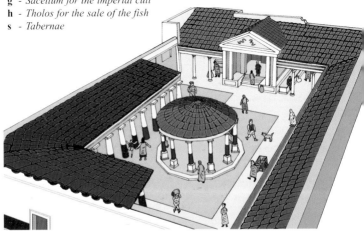

Below, the Temple of Apollo and an hypothesis of reconstruction..

13 Temple of Jupiter

Pompei - Drinking Horn (rhyton).

The temple of Jupiter was founded by the Samnites. After the Roman colonization, on account of its pre-eminent position in the Forum, the political centre of the city, the temple was dedicated also to Juno and Minerva, as in the Roman Capitol, where all three divinities were worshiped. The temple stands on a high podium in the Italic style (like the temple of Apollo). Inside the podium was the favissa, the place where sacred ornaments, votive gifts and probably the city treasure were kept. The altar is on top of the podium, which is incorporated into its stairway. At its sides are found the two equestrian statues depicted in the famous marble relief found in the house of L. Caecilius Iucundus. The pronao (part of the temple that comes before the cell) has a facade of six Corinthian columns; the three niches on the inside are empty, although at the time of the eruption people found many fragments of statues of divinities, some of them of enormous size.

14 Forum Olitorium

A wide rectangular-shaped area located on the western side of the Forum which was used as market for the selling of fruit and vegetables. At the time of the eruption, the building, already damaged by the earthquake of 62 AD, was not completely restored yet. Today, it is used to store the archaeological materials which are found.

"Mensa Ponderaria": marble plate with different holes for the measurements of weight unities.

15 Mensa Ponderaria

Near the Forum Olitorium, in a niche opened in the east wall of the Temple of Apollo, there was the Mensa Ponderaria - a slab of marble with several circular cavities calibrated on the Oscan metric system, as you can infer by the inscriptions inside them, and an opening for the spillage of the measured product at the bottom. Later that metric system was conformed to the one carried out by the emperor Augustus as the epigraph carved on the front of the slab testify.

Steelyards

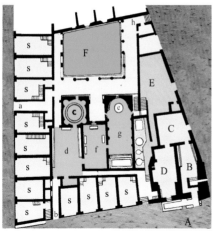

a - *Entry from Via del Foro*
b - *Entry from Via delle Terme*
c - *Male Frigydarium*
d - *Male Apodyterium*
e - *Male Labrum*
f - *Male Tepydarium*
g - *Male Calydarium*
h - *Entry from Vico delle Terme*
s - *Tabernae*
A - *Female entry from Via delle Terme*
B - *Apodyterium and basin of the female Frigydarium*
C - *Female Tepydarium*
D - *Female Calydarium*
E - *Open Area*
F - *Gym*

16 Forum Thermal Baths

These baths – the only ones working at the time of the eruption – had sections for men and women with separate entrances. Going in through the men's entrance from Via delle Terme, after a narrow corridor one enters the dressing room, a big vaulted room with stucco decorations and seats along three sides. At the back of the room there is a passage leading to the frigydarium (cold water pool), a round pool with steps covered by a cupola and an opening in the centre for air and light. Having returned to the dressing room, to the left we find a finely decorated room with a vaulted roof. One can still see the bronze brazier that moderately heated the room and the series of niches that were used to place personal objects and

Statue of a crouched golden-haired child, found in the three side porch of the house of the working Painters. Perhaps it was the terminal part of a garden fountain.

Necklace and couple of earrings found in the villa of Poppea in Oplonti. Naples, National Archaeological Museum.

Part of the Calydarium with the labrum (marble basin from which throws of cool water gushed) with above the opening to convoy the light. Below, the Tepydarium with the terra-cotta telamones to divide the shelves, where the suits were deposed, and the fine polychrome stucco of the vault.

balms in. The niches are separated from one another by figures of giants upholding a plinth, a motif.also found in the roofed theatre. The last room contained the hot bath.

To the right is a pool, and to the left a big marble basin for cold water ablutions and air humidification. On the edge of the basin is an inscription with bronze letters citing the two duumviri who commissioned it (Cneus Melissius Aprus and Marcus Staius Rufus) and the price paid (5250 sestertii). At the back of this room was the furnace that heated the waters and the air that circulated in cavities in the walls and underneath the pavement. The women's section is smaller and also has its entrance on Via delle Terme.

17 Temple of Fortuna Augusta

Excavated from 1823 to 1826. Erected in a east-west direction on the corner of the street of Forum, on which the façade opened, and the Street of Fortune, just a few steps from the Forum. Inside the cella the monument, a prostyle with four columns in the façade and two sides, had niches for statues and an aedicula inserted into an apse, where the simulacrum of the goddess of Fortune, represented with a rudder and a cornucopia, was situated. The white marble inscription on the aedicula shows the following text in two lines: M (arcus) Tullius M (arci) f (ilius) d (uo) v (ir) i (ure) d (icundo) tert (ium), quinq (uennalis), augru, tr (ibunus) mil (itum) a pop (ulo), aedem Fortunae August (ae) solo et peq (unia) sua. "Marcus Tullius, Marcus' son, five-year judging duumvir for three times, augure, military tribune elected by the people, (built) the temple of the Fortuna Augusta on his own land and at his own expense". So, the building fits into the architectural works of "propaganda" supporting the dynasty founded by Augustus M. Tullius, with the Olconi and belonging to one of the most powerful families of the Augustan Pompeii.

Temple of Fortuna Augusta.
Above, the hypothesis of reconstruction.

PLANT OF A POMPEIAN HOUSE

- **a** - *Vestibulum (space in front of the atrium)*
- **b** - *Fauces (Narrow passage)*
- **c** - *Cellae (Little room or barn)*
- **d-n** - *Cubicula (resting room)*
- **e** - *Atrium*
- **f** - *Alae (waiting room in the atrium, near the tablinum, characterised from an opening as wide as all the ambient)*
- **g** - *Tablinum*
- **h** - *Apotheca (provision store)*
- **i** - *Andron (corridor ,passage among walls)*
- **j** - *Triclinium*
- **k** - *Peristilio*
- **l** - *Exedra (wide ambient to live and to have lunch, generally bright and facing the peristyle. In the suburban villas it was located in panoramic position*
- **m** - *Oeci (Living room)*

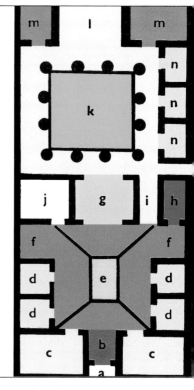

The House

Pompeii was a highly urbanized town; still today when we walk along its streets, we realize that Pompeians exploited all the space at their disposal in a very rational way. Nevertheless, it is necessary to make an effort of imagination in order to reconstruct the original aspect of the old town. At present Pompeian buildings might suggest the idea that Pompeii was a town with low buildings, having only a ground floor. But this is not true, although many of the buildings along Via dell' Abbondanza are, indeed, single-storey. However, before going further, it is necessary to provide you with some facts about the most important rooms of the Pompeian house.

The "atrium" is one of main parts of the buildings. Its main characteristic is the gap in the middle of the roof, which was useful both for giving lights to the rooms which faced the atrium and for allowing the rain to enter into the house, so that it could be gathered on the floor (the **impluvium**), which, in its turn, carried the water to the underlying cistern: this was the most effective system for gathering water for domestic uses, before the introduction of waterworks, which solved the problem of the water supply in a different way. Vitruvius, who wrote a treatise on architecture in the first century B.C., lists different kinds of "atria", which differed according to the roofing: the **Tuscan** roofing (open in the middle and without columns to support the roof); the **tetrastyle** roofing (open in the middle, with four supporting columns); the **Corinthian** roofing (open in the middle and with more than four columns); the **depluviated** roofing (with the pitches of the roof oriented towards the outside; the **testudinate** roofing (without any opening in the middle of the roof). **The "cubiculum"** is a small bedroom, connected to the atrium. **The "tablinum"** is a room that faces the atrium and is usually opposite to the hall. Originally, it was the residential room of the householder and maybe Pompeians consumed their meals in this room; later, it seems that the tablinum assumed just representative functions. **The "peristyle":** the addition of the peristyle to the primitive system of the Italic house is due to the adoption of Hellenistic cultural models by the Roman world. It is a wide garden, surrounded by porticos; very often small statues were placed in it, or it was even decked out like a real art gallery full of historical and mythological characters. These statues had the aim of illustrating the cultural or religious models to which the householder was devoted. In a certain way, within that process of integration between nature and architecture which enjoyed a great success during the Hellenistic period, Pompeians tried to bring into their house a piece of nature, through the creation of gardens decorated with ornamental plants and the play of water.

The "triclinium" is the dining room, in which Pompeians used to place three beds ("klinai" in Greek) on which they would recline in order to have their meals according to a Greek usage adopted in Rome, too. Very often it was open on the peristyle. It had to be two times longer than its width; and in many cases, besides a winter triclinium, we also find a summer triclinium, often built outside.

Reconstruction of the interior of a Pompeian house.

View of the great atrium of the house of the Faun and the impluvium with marmoreal banks and polychrome rhombuses with in the centre the dancing Faun.

18 House of the Faun

This is one of the biggest, most luxurious houses in Pompeii (2,970 square meters). Houses as large and luxurious can only be found only in Pella, capital of the Macedonian kingdom and belonging to the same period, or in Libia and dating back to the Ptolemaic period. We do not know the name of the owner of the house, although we do know that the decorations show a marked Egyptian influence, especially from the

a - *Vestibulum*	**b** - *Tabernae*
c - *Impluvium*	**d** - *Tuscanic atrium*
e - *Tablinum*	**f** - *Cubicula*
g - *Alae*	**h** - *Tetrastyle atrium*
i - *Oecus*	**l** - *Exsedra of*
m- *Culina*	*Alexander's mosaic*
n - *Bathrooms*	**o** - *Triclinium*
p - *Oeci*	**q** - *Minor peristyle*
r - *Large peristyle*	**k** - *Back exit*

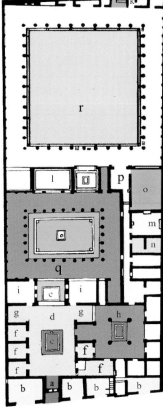

Plant of the House of the Faun

alexandrine milieu. The present plan dates back to the 2nd century B.C., but the house was erected over a pre-existing building. The house takes its name from a small, bronze statue depicting a dancing Faun. The original, of the Hellenistic school, is now in Naples, but a copy can be seen in the centre of the pool in the first atrium. An interesting decoration is found in the small entrance hall, consisting in stucco corbels and columns and in

Mosaic with animals and sea fauna, and a cat that bites a partridge. Naples, National Archaeological Museum.

squares painted in a single colour to simulate marble panels. It is one of the most interesting examples of the first phase in Roman painting, which scholars refer to as "First Pompeian Style". Around the first atrium, of Tuscan type, were various bedrooms. At the back is the tablinum with a lavish pavement adorned with cubes. The skeleton of a woman who had tried to escape with her belongings (jewels and coins) was found here. Around the second atrium (to the right) were the servants' quarters, which were also connected to a small thermal area. Then comes the first peristyle, which has 28 tuff columns covered with stucco. At the back an entrance with two columns leads to a hall. The hall pavement was removed and transported to the National Museum of Naples, in 1832; it contains the famous mosaic of the Battle Between

The great polychrome mosaic that decorated the floor of the exedra of the house of the Faun. Made of over one million of tesserae, it represented the battle of Isso between Alexander Magnus against Dario. Naples, National Archaeological Museum..Since 6 October 2005 a copy of this famous mosaic, made bes and Instruction Center of Ravenna and corresponding to the original measures (metres 3,17 x 5,84 metres), shapes, materials and colours, has come back to adorn the exedra.

Alexander the Great and Darius at Issus. The mosaic, based on a Hellenistic painting, measures 5 meters by 2.7 and is made up of more than a million and half pieces, At the back of this hall is the second peristyle, the largest and more recent one, with 44 Doric columns, two rooms for the gardener at the back to the right, and, to the left, a small lararium.

19 House of the Small Fountain

The house derives its name from the beautiful fountain-cum-nynphaeum which is covered with mosaics of vitreous paste, shells and marble and placed at the back of the garden. The water gushed out from a comic mask, which was on the wall of the apse, and from the mouth of a goose held under the left arm of a bronze amorino.

Patera

Achille and Skyros. Fresco in the House of Dioscuri. Below, the Peristyle

20 House of the Large Fountain

The use of the fountains-cum-nynphaeum became widespread since the half of the 1st century AD. This house, which is next to the previous one, has a fountain with stuccoes and mosaics of vitreous paste and mollusc shells and bronze statues, too. The posts of the fountain were decorated with two tragic masks.

Bronze lamp holder

21 House of the Dioscuri
(House of Castor and Pollux)

The house has one of the few Corinthian atriums with the roof supported by twelve tufa columns. It is famous for its great wall paintings in the fourth style such as *Scylla and Minosse*; *Apollo and Daphne*, *The birth of Adonis*, *The young Silenus and Bacchus*. At the entrance it is significant the painting of the *Dioscuri Castor and Pollux*, which gives its name to the dwelling and is at the National Archaeological Museum of Naples.

The Thermopolium of the house of Sallust with the paintings in the I Style on the external facade of the house.

Pompeian styles and painting

Even today, when we find ourselves before a Pompeian fresco, we can' t help admiring these wonderful combinations of colours and shapes which made the houses of the town particularly lively. But how did they do the frescoes? First they did a guide-drawing (sinopia) on a layer of wet plaster. Later, it was refined with colours or with stucco; the latter was

Caupona of Euxinus - Popular paintings.

particularly used for frameworks and architectural decorations. Then, through a chemical reaction, colours were fixed on the plaster. For this reason, the Pompeian artists decorated the wall, piece by piece, with extreme care; they weren't allowed any mistakes. They couldn't correct them but would be compelled to remove the fresco and paint it again. As for the great mythological paintings of which we can find a lot of repetitions both in Pompeii and in other centres buried by Vesuvio in 79 A.D., they were carried out on the basis of models (they so-called cartoons) which reproduced famous works and circulated among the various shops of decorators and

Fresco of theatrical Mask II Style, Poppea's villa, Oplonti.

*painters. It was really the unique episode of Pompeii and the huge quantity of old paintings we still appreciate today that induced many scholars (starting from the German Mau) to divide Roman painting into four phases, starting from the second century B.C. to the moment of the 79 A.D. eruption: they are the so called "**Pompeian styles**".*

The fist style: *this style, which, first developed in Greece, spread to Italy in the 2nd century B.C. It is characterized by many polychrome panels, sometimes realized by using stucco,*

Fresco in IV style in the shop of Marcus Vecilius Verecundus - A young man carding a tunic and a second one with a cage of rushes on which the clothes were stretched to treat them with the vapour of sulphur to bleach them. Naples, National Archaeological Museum

standing in a Horizontal row like marble slabs. This style is present in the oldest houses of Pompeii (i.e. "The house of Sallust" and "The house of the Faun").

The second style: with this style, dated between 80 B.C. and 20B.C., "breaking" of the wall is realized; from the wainscot there are pilasters and columns that divide the space. In the middle there is a huge painting. Moreover, there are series of paintings with large figures (megalografie) that unfold as friezes on the wainscot-podium (i.e. "Villa of the Mysteries" and "Villa of Fannio Sinistore at Boscoreale") and by the wall that constitutes the background to the figures, separated by architectural elements. **The third style:** this style is dated between 20B.C. and 60A.D. and is characterized by a closing of the wall, which is tripartite horizontally and delimitated by friezes and frameworks. In the middle there is a huge mythological picture and on the side compartments are small isolated figures. **The fourth style:** this style is the last phase of Pompeian painting. There is a mingling of figured pictures and architectural elements. The latter lose their structural functions and become fully ornamental. The peculiarity of this style is the mingling of painting and stucco, used in the decorations both to represent architectural elements and to depict mythological and human figures.

Painting in III style representing an Egyptian divinity. Anubi, the god of the deaths, painted sitting on his legs with the jackal head

Peristyle of the house of Meleager with in the centre a basin fed from a fountain.
Below, the marble cartibulum (table with snout legs) discovered in the atrium.

22 House of Meleager

To the left wall of the entrance hall is a fresco of *Meleager and Atlanta Resting* from which the house (excavated at the beginning of the 19th century) takes its name. In the atrium, near the pool where rain-water was collected, there is a fine marble table. To the left is the entrance to the ample peristyle in the centre of which is a pool with niches. Also opening onto the garden is the beautiful reception room with columns. At the back were the kitchen and servants' quarters.

23 House of Apollo

The house was probably occupied by a merchant, one Erenuleius Comune. The house has two gardens, one with a beautiful pyramidal fountain. There are also mythological frescoes depicting Apollo, who is also represented in a statue set on a pedestal at the side of the tablinum.

24 House of the Tragic Poet

This is a rather small house that takes its name from a mosaic on the pavement of the tablinum (room coming after the atrium and marked by a step) depicting a scene of a tragedy, now in the National Museum of Naples.
At the entrance there is the famous mosaic of a watch-dog and the inscription *cave canem*,

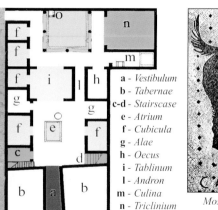

a - *Vestibulum*
b - *Tabernae*
c-d - *Stairscase*
e - *Atrium*
f - *Cubicula*
g - *Alae*
h - *Oecus*
i - *Tablinum*
l - *Andron*
m - *Culina*
n - *Triclinium*
k - *Larario*

Mosaic cave canem, inserted in the floor of the vestibulum.

"beware of the dog". The atrium is of the Tuscan type, which is with a roof supported by beams and without columns in the centre. At the back of the peristyle there is a mall temple-like shrine. In the hall that leads into garden two frescoes can still be seen: *Ariadne Abandoned by Theseus* and a group of Cupids.

25 House of Pansa

The house is also known as *Insula Ariana Polliana* because this is how it is called in an inscription found on the outside, which gave notice that one could apply inside for the rental of shops with an upper floor, luxury apartments and houses. The house dates back to the second half of the 2nd century A.C. and takes up an entire block. It has the same sequence of atrium and double peristyle found in the house of the Faun.

*Food warmer -
Four Styles Housei*

The peristyle of the house of Pansa with a great basin instead of the garden.

26 House of the Bakery

It is one of the largest bakeries among the thirty-five come to light during excavations. In the garden there are four millstones of lava rock on bases, in *opus incertum*. At the back there is the oven for baking bread and the plank supports for making flour.

The house of Sallust with atrium and the tablinum, decorated in the I Style.

Hypothesis of reconstruction of the house of the Surgeon

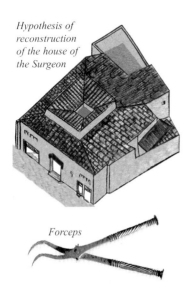

Forceps

27 House of Sallust

The house, among the most ancient ones of Pompeii, perhaps was occupied by *A. Cossius Libanus* as suggested by a signet ring found in 1806. Its Italic-type structure, dating back to the 3rd century BC, consists in a series of bedrooms around the Tuscan atrium and then the tablinum opened onto the vegetable garden which enclosed the house at the back. In the last period also this house will have been converted into a hotel as you can deduce from the inn next to the atrium and from a series of small rooms which must have been on the upper floor. At the end of the garden there is the wall painting of *Actaeon attacked by the goddess Diana's dogs, whom the hunter dared to see naked.*

Fresco in the house of Sirico, portraying the surgeon Iapige while extracting the arrow from the leg of Aeneas.

Box for medicine

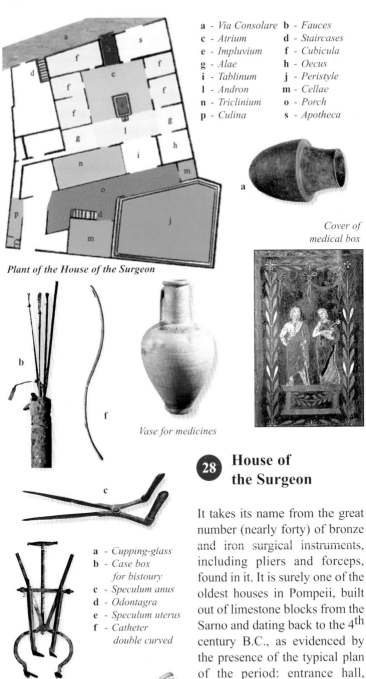

a - *Via Consolare* b - *Fauces*
c - *Atrium* d - *Staircases*
e - *Impluvium* f - *Cubicula*
g - *Alae* h - *Oecus*
i - *Tablinum* j - *Peristyle*
l - *Andron* m - *Cellae*
n - *Triclinium* o - *Porch*
p - *Culina* s - *Apotheca*

Cover of medical box

Plant of the House of the Surgeon

Vase for medicines

a - *Cupping-glass*
b - *Case box for bistoury*
c - *Speculum anus*
d - *Odontagra*
e - *Speculum uterus*
f - *Catheter double curved*

28 House of the Surgeon

It takes its name from the great number (nearly forty) of bronze and iron surgical instruments, including pliers and forceps, found in it. It is surely one of the oldest houses in Pompeii, built out of limestone blocks from the Sarno and dating back to the 4th century B.C., as evidenced by the presence of the typical plan of the period: entrance hall, Tuscan atrium surrounded by bedrooms, tablinum and an orchard to the rear.

29 Porta Herculaneum
and street of Tombs

This gate is situated in the north-western corner of the city. Its ancient name was *porta salis* (in Oscan *veru sarinu*), both meaning "salt gate". This was because it was through this gate that salt was brought in, after being harvested from the Herculaneum salt flats, located along the banks at the mouth of the Sarno river, probably on both sides. Moreover, Porta Herculaneum must also have been used to introduce most of the supplies and goods from the harbour, considering that the only other possible access route, Via Medina, was steep and led to the pedestrian area of the Forum, where vehicular traffic was forbidden. In fact, Via Medina lacks the typical ruts left on the cobbles by the continuous passage of carts. Outside Porta Herculaneum, on both sides of the street of Tombs, the road leading out of the gate, a number of sepulchral monuments with statues and funereal inscriptions were raised after the Roman colony was founded.

A tract of Via delle Tombe.

30 Necropolis of Porta Herculaneum

In the Samnite period (425-80 BC) the Pompeians commemorated their dead with the burial rite. The tombs of this period are at inhumation, nearly all at grave and only one is a chamber tomb. With the beginning of the Roman period (80 BC) the funeral rite of incineration was prevalent. The ashes, gathered in terracotta, marble, and sometimes glass urns, were placed in monumental tombs which could be the niche, chamber, circular mausoleum, semicircular altar or exedra type (schola). The urns were buried behind the front of the sepulchres; while as regards the chamber tombs they were placed in the niches. Another custom was

A view of Porta Herculaneum from Via Consolare. Aside, hypothesis of reconstruction of the ancient door.

The priestess Mami's sepulchre shaped in semicircular seat, at the back the ruins of the mausoleum with columns of the Istacidi, both of Augustan age.

the accompanyment of the deceased in procession as far as their last dwelling, wearing black or dark clothes (toga-pulla). In case of rich persons, the procession was followed by hired mourners, women recruited to lament the pain of the family. They wore some little cruets under their eyes to collect the tears for certifying the authenticity of their crying.

31 Villa of Diomede

This is a suburban villa, quite luxurious. From the street one enters directly into the peristyle, surrounded by 14 columns.

To the left one finds an area where hot baths were located. There is also a quite interesting, semicircular bedroom. On the side opposite the entrance is the triclinium with a beautiful view.

On a lower level, to be reached by a stair, is a vast, square garden surrounded by a cryptoporticus. In the midst of the garden is an open-air triclinium with a pool. In the cryptoporticus the remains of the bodies of 18 victims were found.

A blue glass-cameo vase, discovered in the necropolis of Porta Herculaneum. Now preserved in Naples, National Archaeological Museum.

View of the villa of the Mysteries.

32 Villa of the Mysteries

The Villa was built around the 2nd century B.C. at about 400 meters outside Porta Herculaneum. In the last phase, during the 1st century A.D., the villa was enlarged with a rustic construction and some areas ceased to be used as residential areas, being turned over to the production of farm produce. This is a symptom of the crisis encountered in the management of rich villas under the Flavian emperors, made worse by the severe blow to the economy inflicted by the earthquake in 62 A.D. The main entrance to the villa was from the east, i.e. on the opposite side from where visitors are admitted today. For this reason, it is advisable to start one's visit from the far side in order to have the right idea of the lay-out. On both sides of the area just outside the small room leading into the peristyle, one finds a series of rustic rooms built onto the villa by a certain L. Istacidius Zosimus, probably an overseer hired by the owners. In these buildings there was a wooden winepress and a system of basins, channels and cisterns where the must was gathered.

On the other side of this rustic area there was a latrine and a courtyard with two ovens. In

Urceus for garum

Amphora

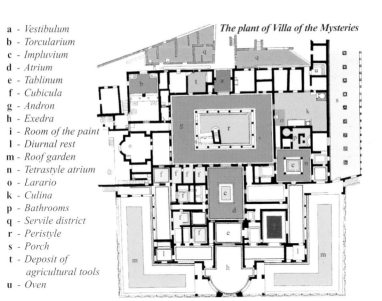

a - *Vestibulum*
b - *Torcularium*
c - *Impluvium*
d - *Atrium*
e - *Tablinum*
f - *Cubicula*
g - *Andron*
h - *Exedra*
i - *Room of the paint*
l - *Diurnal rest*
m - *Roof garden*
n - *Tetrastyle atrium*
o - *Larario*
k - *Culina*
p - *Bathrooms*
q - *Servile district*
r - *Peristyle*
s - *Porch*
t - *Deposit of agricultural tools*
u - *Oven*

the rear, right corner of the courtyard a narrow corridor leads to a small atrium-garden, onto which a small hot-bath area opens; when the eruption took place, it had not been in use for some time. One of the most beautiful decorations in Pompeii is found in a bedroom beyond the Tuscan atrium, to the right of the original entrance. The tablinum, per-fectly in line with the peri-style- atrium axis, has a black wall decoration. To the left of the tablinum is a room with two beds. The walls are fres-coed with sacrifice scenes showing Dionysus, maenads and satyrs, dancing. The room, which made famous the Villa of the Mysteries, is a triclini-um with walls frescoed with a megalographia. The large

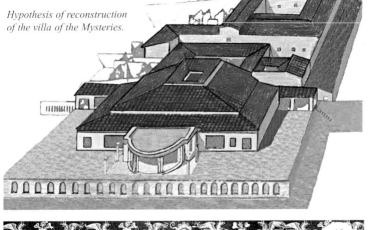

Hypothesis of reconstruction of the villa of the Mysteries.

I   *II*   *III*

frieze contains 28 human figures on a podium. In the background is a series of architectonic motifs on a red wall. The sequence of figures is extremely fetching to the modern eye, almost cinematographic in its effect. Stylistically the fresco belongs to a phase of Roman painting know as the "Second Pompeian Style, done between 80 and 20 B.C. It is fairly sure that the artist who painted the scene (many scholars think he was from Campania) modelled

it on a more ancient Alexandrine original, from the 4th or 3rd century B.C. Not all scholars agree on the meaning of the fresco. The prevailing interpretation is that it represents the initiation of a young woman into the rites of Dionysus, but even within this general agreement there is variance as to the roles and actions of the personages. In the right corner, just after the main entrance, one sees the young woman getting herself

VI   *VII*

IV   V

ready or the initiation, assisted by a handmaid and two cupids. To the left, after the brief space between the main and secondary entrances, we find a seated woman covered with a mantle, who has been identified as either the lady of the house or a priestess of Dionysus. The long wall to the left has 11 human figures. Seen from left to right, the initiate listens to the text of the holy ritual read by a boy (Dionysus as a child?), under the tutelage of a seated priestess. Then a maiden advances with a plate of offerings toward a priestess, seated with her back to the observer, who is preparing a sacrifice, assisted by two adepts. Then there is a pastoral scene with Silenus leaning on a pillar, playing a lyre, and two satyr-like figures: a youth playing a sort of reed flute and a woman nursing a goat. The last figure is a woman, terrified, who shrinks back from the sight of the next scenes,

VIII   IX

Frescoed walls in II style that divides the peristyle from the atrium.

which show the initiative being flogged. Thus, we have come around to the wall facing the main entrance, on which there are eight personages. From left to right, we find a seated Silenus giving wine to a young satyr, while another satyr, at his back seeks to frighten the younger one by reflecting the image of a tragic mask in the cup of wine. Beside these figures, there is the god Dionysus, probably drunk, who lies in Ariadne's lap (the upper part of her body is missing). Then a kneeling initiate, with another figure standing behind her back, is uncovering a phallus, a Dionysian symbol. The last figure, probably a god, is whipping an initiate (we are now looking at the right wall of the room), who is kneeling, supported by a companion.

Finally the young woman, done with the rite of initiation, is depicted as naked and beside herself with ecstasy, in the throes of a Bacchic dance, accompanied by a woman holding the sacred baton.

Wine press and cannulae to test the wine.

Caius Vestorius Priscus' tomb outside the walls of Porta Vesuvio. Below, the Castellum aquae near Porta Vesuvio where the water of the Serino flowed through a branch of the Augustan aqueduct.

33 Necropolis of Porta Vesuvio

Among the monumental tombs of the necropolis outside the walls of Porta Vesuvio, it is particular the tomb of C. Vestorius Priscus, an aedile died at the age of twenty-two years. In order to mean his high status (as public administrator), the interior walls of the tomb were frescoed with episodes from the life of the deceased.

Amulet

34 Castellum Aquae (Water Tower)

This building occupies the highest spot in the city and was a large water reservoir. The water came from the aqueduct of the Serino and was channelled from here in three directions. Moving by gravity the water reached street fountains and public and private buildings. The facade has four pilaster strips and three blind arcades, which serve to identify this building, along with Porta Vesuvio, as the subject of two famous reliefs found in the house of L.Caecilius Iucundus, depicting the 62 A.D. earthquake.

Water Supply

The problem of water in ancient times has always stimulated the research for new solutions and techniques. At Pompeii the problem was solved in the earliest period both by drawing water from the phreatic stratum, by means of deep wells made in the bank of tuff on which the town raises, and by means of a system of domestic

Partition basin of the water inside the Castellum aquae.

Arrest key

gathering. An opening was left in the roof of the atrium, with converging pitches (compluvium) through which rain-water could penetrate to be gathered in a low basin in the underlying floor (impluvium). The impluvium was connected through a

series of openings to an underlying reservoir in which water was stored. Then water was drawn through a sort of well (puteum) made of marble and set on the sides of the impluvium.

Pan-pipe

Later, with the creation of the Roman waterworks, the "Serino", the town was provided with water by a network, which started from the great public reservoir of Porta Vesuvio; from this point water was distributed to the houses and public buildings.

Suction pump

Pump part

House of the Gilded Cupids, the garden with the portico of the peristyle.

35 House of the Golden Cupids

This finely decorated house belonged almost certainly to a member of the Poppaei family related to Nero's second wife, Poppaea. The tablinum had a fresco of *Helen and Paris*. Entering the peristyle one finds oneself in an almost magical atmosphere; next to the 15 Doric columns and in the garden there are a series of hermes, small statues, carved animals, masks, and, hanging from the architrave, medallions against the evil eye.

The rear side of the portico is raised in an exquisite fashion so as to give an illusion of depth. In the left corner there is a sacellum consecrated to three Egyptian divinities: Isis, Serapis and Arpocratis. Continuing along the peristyle, at the rear, we find a dining room with three beds (the triclinium), which was still being restored at the time of the eruption. Following is a bedroom with erotic frescoes: *Actaeon Surprising Diana Bathing*; *Venus Fisherwoman*; *Leda and the Swan*. The next room leads to the kitchen area. Descending the steps and turning left, just after the lararium we find the bedroom whence the house takes its name: in the walls are glass disks with Cupids engraved in gold leaf.

House of the Gilded Cupids, the tabernacle.

The peristyle of the house of the Vettii and below, the plant.

36 House of the Vettii

Names of the owners, Aulus Vettius Restitutus and Aulus Vettius Conviva, are known thanks to two seals found in the atrium. The house has two atria and a beautiful garden. In the entrance hall two fighting cocks and a Priapus are depicted, the latter serving to ward off bad luck. In one of the atria are two strong-boxes on low walls, which presumably served as status symbols. The walls of the atrium were adorned with Cupids, and sacrificial and hunting scenes. In the small room immediately to the left are two frescoes: *Leander Swimming to His Beloved Ero* and *Ariadne Abandoned by Theseus in Naxos*. Next comes another richly decorated hall with frescoes of *Cyparisso*

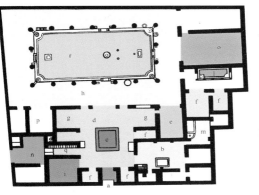

a - *Vestibulum*
b - *Larario*
c - *Impluvium*
d - *Tuscanic atrium*
e - *Triclinium*
f - *Cubicula*
g - *Alae*
h - *Porch*
i - *Oecus*
l - *Viridarium*
m - *Culina*
n - *Stables*
o - *Triclinium - Hall of the cupids*
p - *Oecus*
q - *Staircases*
r - *Peristyle*

Plant of the house of the Vettii

Hypothesis of reconstruction. Below, the Vintner Cupids that decorate the walls of the atrium and the predellas of the saloon.

Turning into a Cypress and Pan Fighting Cupid, and a plinth where Jupiter is depicted in various attitudes. In the second atrium of the villa, which also leads to the servants' quarters, are the stairs that led to the upper floors. Here we have a beautiful lararium with painting of the *Genius of the House Between Two Dancing Lares* above a serpent representing the patron divinity of the house. The kitchen still has five bronze kettles on a tripod and some vases. The small adjacent room was for the cook. It is decorated with three, small, erotic paintings, and houses a statue of Priapus from the garden. Retracing our steps, we enter the garden splendidly decorated with statues of Cupids and putts, with many tables, basins and fountains. In the corner to the right is the dining hall, the triclinium decorated with three large paintings: on the left-hand wall *Daedalus Presenting the wooden Cow to Pasiphae*, at the back *Ixion Tied to the Wheel Built by Vulcan*, to the right *Dionysus Surprising the Sleeping Ariadne Abandoned by Theseus*.

Fresco portraying Hercules strangling the snakes, in the presence of Anfitrione and Alcmena. Below, the fresco of Priapo.

Also opening on the peristyle are a number of halls probably used as female quarters (a gynaecium). Two frescoes remain: *Achilles Recognized By Ulysses* and

Augeas Surprised by Drunken Hercules. Following is an extremely refined reception room, certainly one of the most famous frescoed rooms in the world. The large red panels with missing central paintings are decorated with famous couples from mythology in the act of flying: (from the right) Perseus and Andromeda, Dionysus and Ariadne, Apollo and Daphne, Neptune and Amymone, Hermaphroditus and Silenus. Over the plinth are paintings of Cupids and *psychai* engaged in various activities: (from right to left) *target practice*; *preparing flowers with he-goat to carry roses*; *manufacturing and selling perfumes,*

Fresco, on the left the Supplice of Dirce in the while Anfione and Zeto, after capturing the bull, are going to tie her to it. On the right Penteo the king portrayed while he is killed by the maenads.

Leaving the room we walk along the portico to the right. After the corner there is another reception hall finely frescoed with mythological paintings: (to the right) *Dirce Tied to a Bull by Amphyon and Jupiter*; (in the centre) *Pentheus Slain by the Maenads*; (to the left) *Hercules as a Child Slaying the Serpents Sent by Juno.*

racing four chariots; manufacturing and selling jewels; dyeing; bakers celebrating their patron divinity Vesta; grape-harvesting; triumph of Dionysus; selling of wine. Excellent small paintings are also found beneath the candelabras: *Iphigenia in Tauris*; *Apollo and Diana*; *Agamemnon Sacrificing.*

Cupid riding a crab.

37 House of L. Caecilius Iucundus

The house has the traditional sequence atrium-peristyle. Here were found the two marble reliefs depicting scenes from the 62 A.D. earthquake (area of the Forum and of Porta Vesuvio). In the atrium was a beautifully realistic portrait of Lucius Caecilius, maybe the father of the house's owner, contained in a hermes dedicated by Felix, a freed slave; the bronze original is in Naples, but a copy has been set in its place.

In a room to the rear of the peristyle was found an archive with 154 wax tablets belonging to the owner of the house, the banker L.Caecilius Iucundus; scribbled on them were receipts for various sales and for colonial taxes.

38 House of the Silver Wedding

The house retains the monumental plan of the 2nd century B.C. It is so called because it was discovered in 1893,

Above, the rose peristyle and, below, the Oecus with the four octagonal columns on a square basement and the barrel vault with decorations of II style.

Fresco in the House of the Gold Bracelet..

The great tetrastyle atrium with the rectangular impluvium and the four Corinthian columns in grey tuff.

when Humbert and Margarite of Savoy celebrated their silver wedding. The last owner was L.Albucius Celsus. There is an imposing atrium with four tuff columns, surrounded by bedrooms. The house had two gardens. To the right of the one in line with the atrium there is a complete thermal bath with pool, and to the left a splendid reception room, in the Hellenistic style, with a vaulted roof on four octagonal columns of imitation porphyry, and a fine mosaic pavement.

39 Central Thermal Baths

The construction of these baths began after the 62 A.D. earthquake and was never completed. According to some the choice of the building site (at the crossroads of Via di Stabia and Via di Nola) indicates a gradual shifting of the centre of the city life from the Forum to this area.

The baths were equipped with a cold bath room (also serving as dressing room), a tepydarium and a hot bath room (calydarium) with ornamental niches on the walls. From the calydarium one went into the laconicus, a round hall with four niches that served as a sauna. In the three large halls are a number of large windows looking into the gymnasium at the back where a pool was being constructed.

40 House of M. Lucretius Frontone

The house belonged to this public figure, member of one of the families that moved to Pompeii during the imperial period. The atrium has a fine marble pool to accumulate rain-water and is decorated with large black squares. From here we move on to the triclinium frescoed in golden yellow with a large painting of *Neottolemus Killed by Orestes in Delphi*.

Following is an exquisite small bedroom: to the right *Ariadne Bringing the Thread to Theseus*, and to the left *Venus Having Her Hair Dressed*. The small room that comes next sports the fresco of *Perona Breast-Feeding her Father Micones* and *Narcissus Mirroring Himself in the Waters*. However, the most splendid decorations are found in the tablinum: to the right, *Triumph of Dionysus Accompanied by Ariadne*, to the left the *Wedding of Mars and Venus*. The gardens are also frescoed with hunting scenes.

Atrium and tablinum of M.Lucretius Frontone's house.

Frescoes in the M.Lucretius Frontone's house, above the triumph of Bacchus. Below, the representation of Perona who after overcoming her modesty, nurses her father Micone to save him from starvation during the imprisonment.

41 House of the Centenary

The house is so called because it was excavated in 1879, the eighteenth centenary of the eruption. It had a rather ancient plan (2nd century B.C.) but was renovated during the imperial

Above, an erotic scene. Below on the left, a fresco on the wall of the triclinium: a scene of Euripides' tragedy, Orestes sitting on a pedestal between Ifigea and Pilade. Below on the right, the representation of Bacchus with a luxuriant bunch of grapes with the Thyrsus and the panther next to the Vesuvio; on whose slopes the pompeians cultivated the grapevines. The fertility of the soil is represented from the snake.

period. It has two atria, both without columns. The famous painting of the Vesuvio (now in Naples) was found in the lararium located inside the service atrium. Beyond the atria is the large peristyle with garden and central pool. To the left of the garden were the baths, and at the back one can still see a nymphaeum that contained a statue of Hermaphroditis, with fine multi-coloured mosaics.

Bronze oil lamp

House of M.Obellius Firmus -
the tetrastyle atrium.

42 House of M.Obellius Firmus

The house, whose last owner was M.Obellius Firmus, was still being restored at the time of the disaster. It has limestone walls with parts in tuff, dating back to the Samnite period. The house has a double atrium. One was for reception, with four Corinthian columns, surrounded by small rooms and tablinum. The service atrium is of the Tuscan type, without columns. To the rear is a garden surrounded on three sides by a portico. From the garden one enters a reception room decorated with landscape paintings.

Porta di Nola.

43 Porta Nola
and City Walls

Dug between 1907 and 1908 together with a part of the ring road of the city. It takes the name Porta Nola from the fact that its street led to the Nolan area. The gate with one arch and a tufa barrel vault is decorated with a head of Minerva in the upper part of the arch. During excavaciones an Oscan inscription, attesting that the *meddix tuticus Vibius Popidius* had sponsored the construction of the gate, was found on the facade. The street which led to it was quite steep (that constitued the defensive systems) and was preceded by two ramparts where the walls were inserted.

44 Necropolis of Porta Nola

The widening of the excavations between 1975 and 1978 made resurface three tombs in the outside area of Porta Nola. In particular, the tomb with a quadrangular fence of M. Obellius Firmus, former aedile and duumviri of Pompeii, as you read on the epigraph in the front of the tomb. The other two tombs are the exedra type, of which one has, in the center, a column which support the funeral urn dedicated to *Aesquilia Polla*.

House of the Ancient Hunting,view of the peristyle. Below, detail of the frescoes.

45 House of the Ancient Hunt

Inside this house there are traces of the rich decorations frescoed on the walls of the several rooms. In these rooms you can see mythological small paintings and the big scene of the *wild beast hunting*, painted at the back of the garden. In the tablinum there are decorations of Nilotic landscapes and amorini hunting.

46 Bakery of Popidius Priscus

The bakery was connected to the house in the back, inhabited by Popidius Priscus. Panificio di N. Popidius Priscus Bread was produced in what can only be defined as an industrial fashion, given the number and size of the bakeries. The millstones are interesting. They had two parts: the base was conic and fixed, the top was hollow and biconical, the cone of the base fitting inside it. Grain was poured from above; a wooden

An overall view of the pistrinum (bakery) of Numerius Popidius Priscus with the oven and the stone millstones to grind the flour. Below, a fresco with the representation of a counter for the bread selling.

frame with two side arms was used to rotate the top (usually it was worked by animals) and this caused the grain to slowly descend and be crushed between the two stones, until it emerged as flour, at the bottom, were it was collected. The "assembly line" for bread included a stock of grain, not too big, which was presumably kept on wooden shelves, where there was room also for the flour. The grain was milled and the flour was made into dough and kneaded in metal molds. The dough was baked and set aside to be sold, sometimes even from push-carts.

Wheat millstone

Bread form and carbonized food found in ovens and inns of Pompeii. Typical example is the so called Baker of Modesto, in whose oven remained 81 carbonized forms of bread, baked little instants before the eruption and left with the iron door still closed. (A.Maiuri)

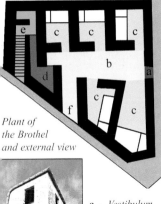

Plant of the Brothel and external view

a - *Vestibulum*
b - *Andron*
c - *Cellae*
d - *Latrine*
e - *Staircases for the top floor*
f - *Secondary entry*

47 Brothel

This is the best preserved brothel in Pompeii. It had ten small cells for prostitutes and customers, five on the upper floor accessible through a separate stairway and equipped with a balcony. The cells on the lower floor had beds of stone on which a mattress was placed. The various erotic paintings have been interpreted as advertisements for the

different "specialties" of the brothel and of the prostitute who worked in each particular room. In the brothel, around a hundred obscene inscriptions have been found, providing us with much information, albeit somewhat crude, on the culture of the period.

48 House of Vedius Siricus

The house includes two dwellings made into one, both with Tuscan atrium and peristyle. It was inhabited by a public figure, P. Vedius Siricus, who had once held the office of duumviro, i.e. city governor. On the pavement at the entrance is the significant writing *salve lucrum*, "welcome profit". Ina room to the left of the atrium, which opened into Vicolo del Lupanare, are mythological paintings: *The Building of the Walls of Troy*, *Thesis in Vulcan' Workshop*, *Hercules with Omphale*.

House of Sirico, fresco. Thetas in the shop of Vulcan.

49 Stabian Thermal Baths

They are the oldest baths of the city. At the moment of the eruption only the female section was functioning, on account of the earthquake. The baths are centred around a large open area, the gymnasium, surrounded on three sides by a portico with tuff columns. To the left is a broad pool, a meter and a half deep, and accessible only from the two lateral halls. The whole area is decorated with multi-coloured stuccos we know to have been made after the 62 A.D. earthquake. The opposite side housed the male and female sections and the separate

a - *Entry from via dell' Abbondanza*
b - *Peristyle - Gym*
c - *Vestibulum*
d - *Male Apodyterium*
e - *Male Tepydarium*
f - *Male Calydarium*
g - *Frigydarium*
h - *Nymphaeum*
i - *Natatio*
l - *Female Apodyterium*
m - *Female Tepydarium*
n - *Female Calydarium*
o - *Praefurmium*
p - *Latrina*
r - *Entry from vico del Lupanare*
k - *Bathrooms*

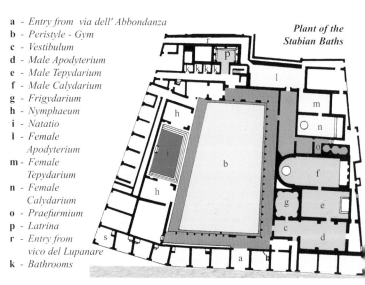

Plant of the Stabian Baths

The apodyterium of the male sector with the vault adorned by polychrome stuccoes. Along the walls there are the clothes - compartments..

quarters where the furnaces were located. These served to heat the pools and the rooms, the latter by causing hot air to circulate underneath the pavements and in cavities inside the walls. The male section can be reached from the lower-right corner of the gymnasium. On the left of the service room is the circular cold bath, while opposite the service room is the dressing room, also decorated with stuccos and equipped with benches and small niches for clothes. To the left, one entered a room heated to a moderate temperature by lukewarm water from a small furnace. Beyond is the hot bath, which is disposed exactly like the one in the Forum baths, with the pool on the short side opposite the entrance and a marble basin for cold ablutions in an apse in the hall. The women's section lacked a cold bath but had all the other facilities. The area opposite the entrance housed the latrines, the old single baths, and a deep well, besides the supervisor's rooms.

Stabian Bath, peristyle (open gym).

Mirror

a - Propylaeums
b - Triangular Forum
c - Porch
d - Fountain
e - Pedestal of Marcellus
f - Doric Temple
g - Grave
h - Tholos
i - Samnite gym
l - Temple of Isis

m - Temple of Giove Meilichios
n - Great theatre
o - Little theatre (Odeion)
p - Four side porch of the gladiators
q - Monumental staircase

Plant of the Triangular Forum

Small statue.

50 Triangular Forum and Doric Temple

The Triangular Forum, so called on account of its shape, lies at the edge of the lava plateau that was once directly over the Pompeii countryside. It must have been quite from the sea and the Sarno river. It is easy to spot the entrance coming down along Via dei Teatri. One enters through a vestibulum that originally had six Ionic columns, three of which remain. The plan, like that of the civic Forum, dates back to the 2nd century B.C., when the imposing portico was built. The latter has 95 Doric columns, which line the open area along two sides. In the centre of the Forum there once was a Doric temple sacred to Hercules, with a tuff base and columns in limestone from the Sarno, at least in the

The Samnite porch of the Triangular Forum, decorated with a marble basin, a honorary base, a round tabernacle and a semicircular seat.

House of the Gilded Cupids. Marble plate where tragic, comic and satirical masks have been carved.

51 Large Theatre

The Large Theatre is in the Greek style and the curve fits the naturally sloping ground. Therefore, the plan has a horse-shoe shape instead of being perfectly semi-circular like all Roman theatres. The theatre was built sometime during the 2nd century B.C. and was renovated many times during the following centuries. One inscription mentions Marcus Holconii Rufus and Marcus Holconii Celer, who, in the Augustan period, had the *cavea* renovated and the two lateral boxes for public authorities as well as the open corridor at the top of the tiers built, all at their own expense. Another memorial tablet records the name of the architect who designed

last phase. Little remains today of the original building, which seems to have been in disuse at the time of the eruption, although the sacred function of the place was probably perpetuated by a small sacellum. The temple is dated from around the year 530 B.C., the same period as the temple of Apollo. It is in the Greek style, with seven Doric columns on its short sides and eleven on the long ones. Later, Minerva also was worshiped there. Other constructions in the Triangular Forum are the following: a base, right after the entrance, that was meant to hold a statue of Macellus, nephew of Emperor Augustus and patron of the city; a semicircular seat to the right of the Doric temple, looking out on the panorama; in front of the temple stairway, a structure identified as the sacrarium of Hercules; a little further on, a deep well once surrounded by a circular building with Doric columns, commissioned by Numerius Trebius.

In the fresco the preparations of an actor before wearing a tragic mask.

the project, Marcus Artorius Primus, something rather uncommon in Roman times. The tiers are semi-circular (this is the part called the *cavea*) and could seat 5000 people. The first four tiers in marble were for the decurions. The entire *cavea* was probably panelled in marble, but the area was subject to pillaging immediately after the eruption. The semi-circular area in the centre of the cavea is called the *orchestra* and had marble panelling. Since it was not used any more for the action (as in the Greek the-

Above, an hypothesis of reconstruction. Below, view of the great Theatre.

Pompeii - Mosaic found in the villa of Cicero representing itinerant musicians. Naples, National Archaeological Museum.

atre), it was converted into an ornamental pool. The scene front is thought to have had two floors originally, only one of which remains. It must have been adorned with many niches, columns, statues and marble panels. In he theatre there was also a statue of Emperor Augustus, in line with the ruling ideology of the Augustan period. A series of stone rings at the top of the *cavea* served to hold poles, which supported an enormous canopy used to shade the spectators from the sun.

Purse

Tibia - musical wind instrument.

52 Small Theatre

The small theatre (or *odeion*, from the Greek) had a very close relationship with the Large Theatre. This is likewise true of ancient Naples, which had an establishment for theatrical productions and a second one for musical

Pompeian fresco with the representation of a young girl granting a little harp, while she is tuning up a cither with the other hand.

Above, an hypothesis of reconstruction. Below, the roofed theatre with the semicircular staircase.

shows. The small theatre of Pompeii was built after the town became a Roman colony (80 A.C.). From inscriptions we know the names of the duumviri who commissioned it, Caius Quintius Valgus and Marcus Porcius, who also commissioned the Amphitheatre.

The *odeion* has a semi-circular plan, with *cavea* cut in order to allow the roof supports to be built.

Here, too, as in the Large Theatre, the first four tiers (in tuff) were reserved for the decurions. The *orchestra* is paved with marble, and at the end of the tiers are two telamones, i.e. two statues of giants, in tuff, upholding two stands. This theatre was used for music, mime and poetry recitals.

Couple of cymbals musical instruments used on dance show and on religious celebrations.

53 Gladiators' Barracks

The garden is surrounded by 74 Doric columns in tuff and measures 46 meters by 33. Originally it was used to accommodate the spectators of the theatre during breaks or when it rained, although it was traditionally a section of the stage.

It was connected to the Triangular Forum through a monumental stairway. In the last phase of Pompeii it became the gladiators' barracks; we know this from the presence of cells and service areas around the portico and by the great quantity of arms, helmets and armours found.

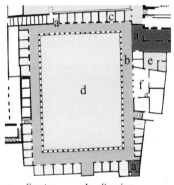

a - *Entries*   **b** - *Porches*
c - *Cells*   **d** - *Gym*
e - *Services*   **f** - *Aula tricliniare*

54 Temple of Jupiter Meilichios

It is a small temple that opens on Via di Stabia.

Helmet, shield and greave worn by the gladiators

There is nothing strange about the fact that there was a temple in a Roman town in Campania consecrated to an Egyptian deity. During the Hellenistic era, religious contacts with the East and Egypt intensified.

The newly imported gods gave the inhabitants of Greece and Italy new reasons of interest and devotion. It is significant that the Temple of Isis in Pompeii was the only sacred building completely restored after the 62 B.C. earthquake, and that the temple of Jupiter, the official temple of the town, was not yet back in service when the eruption \struck. An inscription has preserved the name of the benefactor

The name Meilichios means "as sweet as honey", "kind", and derives from an inscription in Oscan found at the Porta di Stabia.

Meilichios was an ancient divinity, of Greek origin, related to the other early Pompeiian gods, Apollo and Hercules. The temple has a small portico supported by two columns.

Then comes the area in tuff located in front of an Italic-type podium with a stairway and a cell at the top.

Sistrum - Metallic musical instrument that uttered thanks to some movable elements sliding into the holes. Especially used for the cult of Isis.

Fresco coming from Pompeii in which the cult of Isis is represented. Naples, National Archaeological Museum.

who officially reconstructed the Temple of Isis after the earthquake; it was a child of six years, Numerius Popidius Celsino, who, clearly thanks to his father, was welcomed into the order of the decurions. The temple stands on a high, Italic-type podium, with four columns along the façade, to which one ascends by a stair made of masonry. No ritual statues were found in the cell, but some marble fragments probably belonging to a statue of Isis were uncovered in the meeting room behind the temple. The two niches on either side of the cell, in the façade, contained statues of other deities linked with the Isis cult. The podium and cell are surrounded by a portico. In a corner, opposite the entrance, there is an area without a roof, from which a stairway led down to an underground vault where, in a basin, the sacred water of the Nile was kept.

On a pedestal in the opposite corner, at the rear of the cell, was located the famous, ancient-style statue of Isis dedicated by Lucius

View of the temple of Isis. Above, an hypothesis of reconstruction.

Samnite gymnasium.

Caecilius Febus, now preserved in the National Museum of Naples, along with two others: a marble Venus and a bronze portrait of a well-known Pompeii actor, Caius Norbanus Sorice.

Fresco discovered at the back of the temple, where the myth of Io is portrayed. Io was persecuted from Era, because of her love with Zeus, he sheltered in Egypt in the sanctuary placed on the Canapo rock, where the goddess Isis was waiting for her with the cobra in her hand and the crocodile under her feet. Naples, National Archaeological Museum.

56 Samnite Gymnasium

This edifice from the 2nd century B.C. is called *palaestra* (gymnasium) because a marble copy of Polycletus's Doriforus was found there, now in Naples. Given the lack of room, it is likely to the triangular forum. The gymnasium may have been the recognized seat of the military association charged with official functions and award-giving ceremonies. The portico has only three sides. The fourth having been demolished after the earthquake in 62 B.C., when the Temple of Isis, standing to the rear of the Samnite gymnasium, was restored and enlarged.

Clay water-bottle

The median peristyle - House of the Citharist

57 House of the Citharist

This big building, probably owned by the Popidii family, was made out of two previous dwellings. It gets its name from the fact that in one of the three peristyles, the middle one, a lovely, bronze statue of *Apollo Citharist* was recovered, now at the Museum in Naples. Also in Naples are many of the paintings, detached from the walls, and some bronze and marble portraits, among which one representing Marcellus, Augustus' nephew and patron of Pompeii.

House of L.Ceius Secundus - Tetrastyle atrium

58 House of the Ceii

The denomination of *L. Ceius Secundus* was chosen among the nine names mentioned in the electoral posters painted on the façade of the house. It is a small residence but of noble appearance; the ancient front, with a tall door framed by columns with Samnite capitals, is covered with stucco imitating the *opus quadratum*. The vestibule with the painted ceiling closed with a triple-leaf door which opened onto the tetrastyle atrium. A staircase with a wall in *opus craticium* led to the upper floor, which was under construction at the time of the eruption. The walls of the several rooms are frescoed with paintings of Nilotic subjects in the third style. The wall of the garden in the winter triclinium is frescoed with a big hunting scene.

House of L.Ceius Secundus. Hunting scene painted on the wall of the garden.

A razor (Novacula) from a closet of the house of L.Ceius Secundus. (Matteo Della Corte)

House of Menander, view of the peristyle and the atrium with the wall paintings in IV Style.

The representation of the poet Menander.

59 House of Menander

It is one of the houses that has yielded the largest number of everyday objects, as well as two small treasure hoards. It is thought to have belonged to the Poppei family. It gets its name from a fresco showing the poet Menander seated in a rectangular area at the back of the peristyle. In the lower, right-hand corner of the atrium is a lararium.

To the left is a room frescoed with scenes from the Trojan War: to the left, *Cassandra Resisting Ulysses's Abduction*; in the centre, *Cassandra Objecting to the Trojan Horse*; to the right, *Laocoon with His Sons Strangled by the Serpents.* The lower right-hand corner of the room opening out unto the peristyle has some interesting decorations, containing centaurs. In the centre of the pavement is a mosaic with Nile scenes. In the area to the right of the peristyle was the bath and heating area, with decorations. It was heated by a furnace, located in an underlying room, which was also used to cook bread. In the lower room a chest was found with 118 pieces of silverware and a small coffer containing jewels and coins.

Bronze and wood bed discovered in the house of the Menander.

Fresco of the Alae portraying the capture of Cassandra after the Greeks had entered into Troy. Below, mosaic in the calydarium where a fisherman, a swimmer and some fish appear around an acanthus tuft.

Returning to the peristyle, in the rectangular room to the right one finds a small shrine where there were four images of ancestors that were venerated as protectors of the home (plaster-of-Paris moulds were made of these images). Beyond the shrine with Menander there is a semicircle decorated with a painting representing the myth of Actaeon. Moving on into the reception room, one finds the skeletons of some Pompeians who returned to recover some objects after the eruption only to die in the course of the visit. A short corridor leads from this room to the service area of the villa, where there was a stall, cells for slaves, and storerooms for amphoras. In the room near the service entrance a series of bronze farm tools and a handful of coins, as well as the body of the watchman lying on a bronze bed.

Love of Mars and Venus. Silver cantharus coming from Menander's house. Naples, National Archaeological Museum.

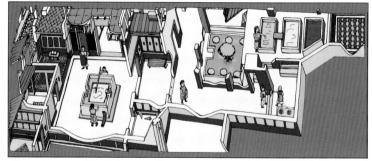
Reconstruction of the Fullonica of Stephanus.

60 Fullonica of Stephanus

Stephanus is one of the characters whose name shows up in the election slogans painted on the façade of the building. In this shop, called a *fullonica* (laundry), robes and tunics were cleaned and the finishing touches were put on cloth and fabrics. The laundry was installed in a dwelling on Via dell' Abbondanza, preserving the earlier structure. At the entrance there was a machine to press tunics. The basin in the atrium was used for washing the fabrics. What had been the peristyle now contained three basins. On the side walls

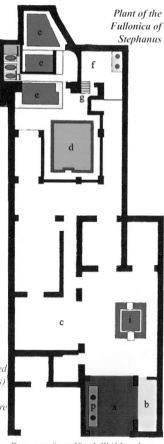

Plant of the Fullonica of Stephanus

Warm-beverage (savomar). House of the Floral Cubicles.

a - *Entrance*
b - *Ostiary*
c - *Atrium*
d - *Peristyle*
e - *Big Basins*
f - *Kitchen*
g - *Staircases*
h - *Ovoidal basins saltus fullonici (stained clothes they were crushed from the workers)*
i - *Impluvium turned into basin for more delicate clothes*
l - *Latrines*
p - *Press*

Entrance from Via dell'Abbondanza

of the middle basin five smaller basins can be seen, in which the fabrics would be crushed underfoot in water along with other liquids, including urine. The urine was kept in three containers alongside the five small basins. Finally, there was a kitchen in the laundry, along with a latrine and a small garden with a portico. The fabrics were hung up to dry on the upper storey.

House of the Cryptoporticus, the larario.

61 House of the Cryptoporticus

The house takes its name from a covered, semi-interred corridor located toward the rear of the dwelling, lit by a series of windows, know by the colourful name of "wolf-snout windows", which opened onto the garden. It was not completely restored after the earthquake, and the owners made use of only one wing as a wine-cellar, where some sixty amphoras were recovered. Although the structure was no longer used as a covered corridor but as a wine-cellar or storage area, without any need for wall decorations, some

Fresco of the oecus with male and female hermae of maenads on pedestal that sustain the shelves of a lacunar ceiling and still-life small pictures.

of the original paintings have been preserved, depicting episodes from Homer. The left wing of the corridor was rebuilt as a hot water system with various rooms for baths, heated rooms and dressing rooms.

The whole house was undergoing reconstruction at the time of the eruption.

 **House of the Lararium of Achilles**

(*House of the Iliac Sacellum*)

After the earthquake of 62 AD, the house of the Lararium of Achilles and the Cryptoporticus one, which, over the centuries had been joined or separated as a result of changes of ownership, were divided again. Today

Atrium of the Lararium of Achille's house.Below,the fine polychrome stuccos of the vault of the Iliac Sacellum.

the signs of the building interventions required for the division are still visible. After the division, the two houses preserved the different level of wealth which had characterized them in the former period. The so-called Iliac Sacellum was the little room where, in a putty frieze on a blue background, was represented a replica from the Trojan cycle showing the preparation and outcome of the last duel between Hector and Achilles. Probably that little room was used for the celebration of family cults.

 ### 63 House of Iulius Polybius

Coming back to Via dell' Abbondanza, we are right in front of Iulius Polybius' s house. Passing through an atrium with no opening in the roof, one enters into another Tuscan atrium, with a rainwater basin made out of an impermeable conglomerate of

Decoration of the feint door.

Porch of the peristyle and below some details of the frescoes.

limestone, sand, pieces of brick and Shingles. A corridor to the left leads to the kitchen, whereas straight ahead the way leads to a garden with a portico. In the lower, left-hand corner there is a bed-room with mythological scenes: *Pasiphae and the Wooden Cow*, *The Judgment of Paris*, *The Goddess Athena with the Serpent Erittonius*. In the room directly opposite this one, beyond the portico, we find still another hand-some fresco, *Dirce Tortured*.

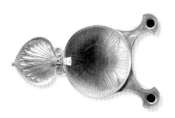

*Oil-lamp of gold,
found in the Temple of Venus.*

64 Thermopolium of Vetutius Placidus

Particularly significant are the many "thermopolium", similar to our modern day cafes, where hot and cold drinks were served; also noticeable is the presence of inns where food and lodging was provided. Their high number confirm the fact that the city was often frequented by foreigners, mainly traders from other towns, both near and far, but there were also occasional visitors attracted by the numerous sports and theatrical events, not to mention the many prostitutes offering all sorts of carnal pleasures, as shown by the crude paintings found in a brothel.

Thermopolium of Vetutius Placidus and above, an hypothesis of reconstruction.

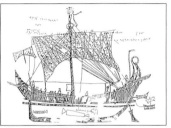

House of the Ship Europa. Reconstruction of the graffito found on the northern wall of the peristyle.

65 House of the Ship Europa

It is called this way for the graffito discovered on the northeastern wall of the peristyle, depecting a cargo ship with the writing: EUROPA. In the large garden of the house, recent

House of the Ship Europa.
The garden.

66 Garden of the Fugitives

excavations brought to light the roots of a vegetable garden with legumes, onions, cabbages and even cherry, peach, apricot, pistachio and lemon trees (particularly used for making medicines, deodorants and rinsing one's mouth).

In a large area cultivated as a vineyard, the plaster casts of thirteen family members, among adults and children, struck by soffocation and terror while they were trying to run away from the violence of the eruption of 79 AD, are grouped.

The tragic death of the Pompeians is testified by the casts obtained by filling the empties produced by the organic decomposition of the bodies. The manager of the excavations G.Fiorelli applied this technique in the 1870. Above, group of casts of persons who were smothered by a rain of ash and lapilli, which were found near a wall surrounding a garden.

67 House of the Garden of Hercules

In the large garden, near the summer triclinium with big brick beds, there is a great lararium with an altar in front of it for votive offerings and the little statue of Hercules, which gives its name to the house.

In this area you can see even the rests of a kennels and some big "dolia" (terracotta jars) for an efficient irrigation system.

The analysis of the garden has confirmed that the land was used to produce olive oil and grow flowers suitable for making perfumes. During excavations they found several terracotta vases for putting little plants, such as cedar and lemon ones, and a big brick seedbed.

The discovery of intact or fragmented, glass or terracotta, containers scattered everywhere, attests that the preminent activity was the production of essences and perfumes.

68 House of Octavius Quartio
(House of Loreius Tiburtinus).

The main entrance to this house, a good example of luxury architecture, is on Via dell' Abbondanza. There is a marble pool in the atrium. The atrium leads on to a *cubiculum* and, to the left, the kitchen.

Behind the atrium is a little garden surrounded by a portico. In the right corner there is a sort of sacellum, probably sacred to Isis, with splendid Paintings (*Diana and Actaeon Tortured*)

The vine-trellis with the transversal channel and in the background, the tabernacle with two great paintings.

and a picture of a priest. When it was discovered, this shrine was empty. To the right of the little garden there is an elegant area, decorated with two friezes, where guests were received.

The upper frieze shows Hercules, the lower one Achilles. Hercules is depicted on the centre wall. On the outside walls one can see Orpheus and Venus. Next, one comes upon a T-shaped channel, the top of the "T" parallel to the house, while the longer channel runs across the whole of the large garden that takes up all the rest of the block. The shorter channel was lined with Dionysian and Egyptian religious statuary. Toward the rear there was a shrine with a fresco, *Narcissus Mirroring*

The tabernacle with two great paintings, on the left Narcisio looking at himself into the water, on the right, Tibse who killed herself on the dead body of Piramo. Above, the hypothesis of reconstruction.

The fountain in the centre of the "euripo" (channel), formed by a square structure from which some little stairs branched-of;the water flowed along them.

Himself in the Waters, to the left, and another fresco, *Thisbe*, to the right. At the juncture between the two parts of the T-shaped channel there was a nymphaeum, over which rose a shrine on four columns. The channel, which probably contained different varieties of fish, is about 50 meters long. There were some basins located along its course, and a wooden portico ran alongside it. Large trees and ornamental plants also grew in the garden.

The philological reconstruction of the vine-trellis with the replanting of the original arboreous essences.

69 House of Venus in the Shell

The most interesting part of the house is the Peristyle with the porch that develops on two sides of the garden. On the background is a great pictorial composition with Venus, in the centre, ploughing the waters within a great shell accompanied by two cupids.

On the sides a paint of Mars and other pictorial compositions with hedge, bloom bushed, marmoreal basins with doves.

Above, Venus. In the centre, the peristyle and below the representation of Mars and floral paintings.

On the left, view of the Great Gym built in Augustan age (27 B.C. - 14 A.C.) consti-tuted by a rectangle of 141 by 107 metres with porticoes on three sides and, the fourth side facing the amphitheatre marked by three monumental entries. In the centre of this rectangle is a swimming pool of 34,55 by 32,25 metres, with a progressive depth till to reach the measure of 2,60 metres, fed from the public aqueduct.

70 Large Gymnasium

This is one of the largest buildings in Pompeii. It was built in the Augustan era to house young men' s associations founded by the Emperor as part of the propa-ganda of his regime. There, the youths engaged in athletics,

which included swimming in the 35 by 23 meter pool in the centre of the field. An imposing portico runs around three sides of the area, with 48 columns on the long side and 35 each on the short sides. Plaster-of-Paris moulds document the existence of a dou-ble line of plane-trees flanking the three sides of the portico.

In 1936, during the excavations supervised by Matteo Della Corte, a famous graffito student, an intact palindrome engraved on a column of the Palestra, near the Amphitheatre, was found. In 1925 another incomplete one, was discovered in the house of P. Paquius Proculus, in via dell'Abbondanza, but its text was not interpreted well. Some believe that the palindrome was a stratagem of the first Christians to hide the sign of the cross, others believe that it was an esoteric, lucky amulet.

View of the Amphitheatre. Below, an hypothesis of reconstruction.

71 Amphitheatre

Two inscriptions on travertine slabs, remind the names of its constructors, the duumviri C. Q.Valgus and M. Porcius, the same who built the Odéion.

The Roman Amphitheatre, which dated back around 70 BC and had a seating capacity of approximately 20,000 spectators, was used for gladiator battles. For its construction it was used the southeastern zone

Fresco, found in the house of Actius Anicetus, representing the bloody fights broken out in Pompeii between its inhabitant and the "Nucerini" spectators.

A brawl between the supporters of opposite couples of gladiators was the spark that caused the ancient resentment between the two communities, originated from contrasts started because of an allotment of earth in Nuceria, which was thought unfair from the Pompeians. Following this events, Nero interdicted the games for ten years. In the paint the velarium that covered the amphitheatre is portrayed. Naples, National Archaeological Museum.

of the city. The *cavea* was divided into three sectors, the ima cavea (the first row) reserved for important people, the *media cavea* and the *summa*. The upper zone of the circular stand could be reached by four outside staircases; two with a double flight which was supported by the archs in the west front of the building, and the other two (with one flight) were at the point of contact between the building and the walls. A system of arcades assured a quick, orderly flow of spectators, through the crypt (the vaulted arcade) beneath the lower seats of the *media cavea* and accessible by four corridors. The cavea was separated from the audience by a tall wall decorated with athletic scenes which are not visible today.

Two "basolato" corridors, which led from the extremities of its longer axis straight to the arena, were used for letting the entrance of gladiators and wild beasts, and also the passage of chariots. Both corridors had small rooms used as *spoliarium* for the first aid to the injured and as mortuary room for the dead. At the external top of the amphitheatre a series of stone

Glass unguentariums in different forms where were contained the oils and the ointments with which the athletes cleansed their bodies before the competition.

rings, inserted into the brick wall, served to support the poles to which was tied, by a system of ropes and pulleys, a big awning for covering the building when the days were too sunny: that service was publicized in the inscriptions painted on the walls of the city and announcing the performances: *vela erunt*, that is "it will be the big awning ". In 59 AD the violent riot, remembered by Tacitus, which broke out between the fans from Pompeii and Nuceria, caused the Roman Senate to decide the closing of the amphitheatre for the next ten years (that resolution was revoked after the earthquake of 62 AD).

72 Porta Nocera and the Necropolis

The ancient, one-arched, barrel-vaulted Porta Nocera built, in *opus incertum*, with the Vesuvian lava stone, stands stately above the street level. Sideways, there are ruins of the mighty walls constructed with blocks of limestone and tufa. Next to the "basolato" street, which led from Pompeii to the neighbouring Nuceria Alfatena, several monumental tombs of families belonging to different statuses were found.

It seems that there were not particular rules to observe for the construction of the graves so they tried to build the tomb in a privileged position in comparison with the others for hiding them.

Above on the left, Porta Nocera with the necropolis.
Above, the Flavii's tomb marked by a façade with several niches. Below, the freedman Pubblius Vesonius Phileros' tomb, in which there are three tuff statues representing respectively the dead person, his mistress and his false friend.

Sacred Pompeii

The sanctuary, designed by Antonio Cua, was consecrated to the Lady of the Rosary in May 1891. Its foundation was possible for the untiring work of the Blessed Bartolo Longo. Lawyer of Latiano, Brindisi, he had come to Pompeii in 1872 to deal the ownership of the countess De Fusco, that married in 1885. In the meantime, he began an intense activity to popularise the Christian religion founding the brotherhood of the Holy Rosary that gathered in the small church of the SS. Salvatore. He promoted a campaign, denominated "a penny a month", with the population to build a great church to devote to the Lady of the Rosary. The façade of the Sanctuary made of travertine by project of the architect Giovanni Rispoli, was completed in 1901. The monumental statue of the Virgo of the

Rosary, carved in a unique block of marble of Carrara by Gaetano Chiaramonte, is on the top. The façade has an atrium with three arcades in the inferior part, while in the superior one, in the centre, the papal loggia decorated with two granite columns is set. The five levels bell tower, carried out on a project of Aristide and Pio Leonori, in 1925, is made of grey granite and white marbles. On the top is a bronze dome surmounted by a

The blessed Bartolo Longo. Aside, the Major Altar. Below, the organ with sculptures and wood carvings covered with pure gold.

cross in copper and bronze with gems. The interior of the Sanctuary is shaped in a Latin cross with three naves, the central one is dominated by an enormous dome high 57 metres. The walls are decorated by polychrome marbles and frescoes that illustrate the facts and the history of the Sanctuary. In the centre of the altar is the picture of the Virgo of the Rosary with the Child and at her sides are Saint Domenico and Saint Catherine from Siena. The paint, contained in a bronze frame is surrounded by the 15 mysteries of the Rosary painted by Vincenzo Paliotti. Unusual is the origin of the picture. It was

Paint of the Lady of the Rosary after the restoration made in Rome in 1965.

bought by the Priest Alberto Maria Radente of the convent of Saint Domenico Maggiore by a second hand dealer of Naples, that gave it to Bartolo Longo. The transport to Pompeii was effected from a carter on a wagon charged with manure. When, it was know that a young woman had recovered from epilepsy after praying the Lady, the picture became cult object of the popular devotion all over the world. On the eight of May and on the first Sunday of October the supplication to the Madonna written by Bartolo Longo is recited. He also started the realization of a series of social and religious works to

The historical arrival of the Pope Giovanni Paolo II, in the excavations of Pompei. Below, the Pope in Bartolo Longo place.

to the Hòly See, the Sanctuary has become Pontifical Basilica. The founder died on October 5, 1926 at the age of 84 years, and he was proclaimed Blessed in October 1980 by Pope John Paul II; who visited Pompeii on October 21, 1979 and on October 7, 2003.

The stele monument raising in front of the Sanctuary is dedicated to Bartolo Longo, and it was built in 1962 by Domenico Ponzi.

give assistance to the poor men, to the orphans and to the children of the prisoners such as the female orphanage, the valley typography, the hospice for the daughters of the prisoners, the worker houses, the hospice for the children of the prisoners. Following the transfer of all the works made by Bartolo Longo

Have contributed to the realization of this work:
Umberto Cesino, Valeria Alfano,
Carlo Manfredi, Carlos Alberto Sertà.

Publishing coordination
Domenico d'Oriano

The publisher is a disposal (of people who reclaim the rights) to regard the iconographic sources that have not been individualized.

© Copyright 2006 by d'Oriano Editore srl
Via Armando Diaz, 18   80045 POMPEI (NA)
Tel. (+39) 081 863 10 10 Fax 081 863 75 56
E-mail:
doriano@dorianoeditore.it - pompeidoriano@infinito.it
www.dorianoeditore.it

ISBN 88-89716-11-8